C000132640

1 MONTH OF
FREE
READING

at
www.ForgottenBooks.com

By purchasing this book you are
eligible for one month membership to
ForgottenBooks.com, giving you
unlimited access to our entire
collection of over 1,000,000 titles via
our web site and mobile apps.

To claim your free month visit:

www.forgottenbooks.com/free948045

ISBN 978-0-260-43411-1
PIBN 10948045

Popular Government

Published by Institute of Government

CHAPEL HILL, N. C.

| VOL. 5 | JUNE, 1938 | NO. 6 |

Courses of Instruction and other services

offered by the

Institute of Government

to the

Officials, Teachers, and Citizens

of the

Cities, Counties and State of North Carolina

Editors

ALBERT COATES

HENRY BRANDIS, JR.   T. N. GRICE
DILLARD S. GARDNER   HARRY W. McGALLIARD

Institute of Government Laboratory Building

The Institute of Government building, pictured on the opposite page, located on Franklin Street, facing the University campus, with four floors and twenty rooms, will house the governmental demonstration laboratory, training schools, library and clearing house of governmental information, clubrooms for officials, Institute staff offices and miscellaneous services.

The governmental demonstration laboratory will be housed in the Institute building. Members of the Institute staff during the past five years have been going from city hall to city hall, county courthouse to county courthouse, state department to state department, collecting, classifying and comparing the different methods and practices in use. These materials constitute the beginnings of a central demonstration laboratory to which successive generations of officials, citizens, teachers and students of government may go to see demonstrated in one place the methods and practices in government they would now have to go to hundreds of places to find. With the help of this laboratory public officials may raise the standard of governmental performance by lifting the poorest practices to the level of the best.

Training schools will be held in the Institute building. Starting with the convention programs of official groups, the Institute staff in the last five years has developed systematic courses of instruction for public officials in the fields of criminal law, taxation and finance, administration of justice in the courts, and in the legal and governmental aspects of public works, safety, health, welfare and relief. These training schools will be extended during the coming year to public affairs committees of citizens' organizations and to teachers and students of civics and government.

The library and clearing house of information will be centered in the Institute building. Books, pamphlets, special studies, maps and charts in the governmental library and clearing house number in the thousands, with hundreds of new studies being added to this collection each month. Nearly 200 governmental magazines from all sections of the country and 150 daily and weekly papers from all sections of the state are regularly coming in with information on current developments in all fields of governmental activity for the use of officials, citizens, teachers and students of government in the schools.

Clubrooms and facilities for housing as many as fifty people will be provided in the Institute building. These rooms will be available to officials, public affairs committees of civic organizations, teachers and students of civics and government attending training schools, conferences, consultations with the Institute staff, and using the laboratory, library and clearing house information.

Institute staff offices will be housed in the Institute building, where ready access to the governmental laboratory, library and clearing house of information will facilitate handling inquiries, and holding consultations with officials and other groups interested in governmental affairs.

Table of Contents

POPULAR GOVERNMENT, the journal of the Institute of Government, is published at Chapel Hill, N. C., 10 times a year—monthly except February and March. Editorial, business and advertising address: Box 990, Chapel Hill, N. C. Subscriptions, per year: $2.00. Single copies, 25 cents each. Advertising rates will be furnished on request. Editor, Albert Coates; Associate Editors, Henry Brandis, Jr., Dillard Gardner, T. N. Grice, and H. W. McGalliard. Managing Editor and Business Manager, H. W. McGalliard. Address all communications to Box 990, Chapel Hill, N. C. Entered as second-class matter at the Post Office at Chapel Hill, N. C. Copyright 1938 by the Institute of Government. All rights reserved.

Institute of Government

HISTORICAL SKETCH

In 1887 a small group of firemen laid the foundation for a North Carolina Firemen's Association. In 1908 a small group of county commissioners organized the North Carolina Association of County Commissioners. During the next two decades other groups of public officials followed these examples. In May, 1932, three hundred representatives of all groups of city, county, state and federal officials in North Carolina came together in the North Carolina Association of Governmental Officers. Representatives of civic and professional groups of men and women and of teachers and students of civics and government in the schools accepted invitations from the officials to join them in studying their government. In September, 1932, six hundred officials, citizens, teachers and students of civics and government in the schools united in forming and participating in the first formal sessions of the Institute of Government "for continuous comparative studies of the structure and workings of government in the cities, the counties and the State of North Carolina—the results of these studies to be set forth in guidebooks, demonstrated in laboratories, taught in schools for public officials, public affairs committees of civic organizations, teachers and students of civics and government."

GROWTH

The Institute's growth may be illustrated (1) by the expanding scope of its work—from administration of the criminal law, to taxation, to finance, to courts, to health and welfare and relief, to public works, to election laws and practices, to legislative practice and procedure, to federal, state, local relationships, to other miscellaneous governmental activities; (2) by the growing attendance from 300, to 600, to 1,000 in its statewide meetings, to double that number in its district meetings of specific groups; (3) by the evolution of the two-day convention into the five to ten-day training school with its systematic curriculum and governmental texts; (4) by the increase of its library and clearing house of information till it includes over five thousand current periodicals, texts, pamphlets and special studies covering different phases of government; (5) by the increasing number of guidebooks in use in city halls, county courthouses and state departments; (6) by the expansion of its headquarters from a private office, to a series of basement rooms, to a rented house, to its laboratory building with four floors and twenty rooms including assembly hall, exhibit rooms, offices and clubrooms for officials.

GOVERNMENTAL LABORATORY

In North Carolina 100 counties, around 300 cities and towns, and a score or more of state departments are doing similar things in different ways, with some ways better than others. Improvements in government and its administration are constantly arising out of the initiative and resourcefulness of officials in city halls, county courthouses and state departments. To illustrate: A county official improved tax listing methods to the point that four thousand new taxpayers and five million dollars in unlisted property were placed on the tax books in one year to lighten the load on those already there. A city official reorganized his tax collecting machinery, improved its operations and cut down the cost of operations $6500 annually. A state official simplified the accounting systems of one governmental agency and cut in half the cost of annual audits. Another official saved the cost of his salary by improved methods in the administration of his office. Some local units have worked out methods of collecting 95% of the taxes while some others collect as low as 50%. These methods and practices to the units making them are worth their weight in gold. To other units they might be worth the same.

Members of the Institute staff during the past five years have been going from city hall to city hall, county courthouse to county courthouse, state department to state department, collecting, classifying and comparing the different methods and practices in use. To illustrate: In one county authorities take a hundred forty-two successive steps in the process of tax listing, assessing and collecting. Some form, blank or record illustrates each successive step. One member of the Institute staff has collected copies of the forms used in each successive step, filling them out as they are filled out in practice to show their uses, attaching a typewritten sheet or more of explanation to each form, with the purpose of giving a concrete demonstration of the successive steps in the process of tax administration. Other members of the Institute staff have followed the same plan in the fields of Criminal Law Administration, Court Administration, Finance and Accounting Administration, Welfare, Health and Public Works Administration, Federal, State and Local Relationships. As these materials are gathered from every office in every city hall, county courthouse and state department, they will lay foundations on which the public officials of North Carolina can raise the standard of governmental performance by lifting the poorest practices to the level of the best.

Training School Courses

The need for training in our governmental personnel has grown out of the fact that we are committed to the theory and practice of elective officers, short terms in office and rotation of officers. This means that every two years hosts of newly elected officials take office in the cities, the counties and the state of North Carolina—too often knowing too little about the powers, duties, and administration of their offices—learning as they go. When their terms end, they are replaced by others who pick up the threads of administration not where their predecessors left off but almost if not quite where they began. Popular government, like the frog in the well, goes forward three feet and falls back two. Accumulated governmental knowledge goes over the wheel to waste. Government is forever in the hands of beginners who do not always have beginners' luck. This is costly training for which the people pay—not in the beginning but in the end. Private business, operating in this fashion, would go broke before beginners learned their business. Public business likewise may go broke before beginners learn their government.

Within the limits of our governmental experience we have seen the political pendulum swing the balance of power from the king to the subject; from officers appointed by the crown to officers elected by the people; from the continuity of long-time tenure to the rotation of short-term officers; from the belief that the common man could do nothing to the belief that he can do anything; from the naive notion of birth as the entitlement to office to the equally naive notion of birth as a qualification for it; from the aristocratic notion that some men are born to fill an office to the democratic notion that all men are born knowing how to fill it; from the antiquated notion that some men are not as good as other men to the current notion that every man is as good as every other man and better.

Within that span of time we have lived to learn that the Commonwealth may be plundered by favorites of the people as well as by favorites of the king; that "to the victor belongs the spoils" may be alike the doctrine of hereditary rules and elected officeholders; that shades of ancient spoilsmen may still gather in the modern sheriff's eyes; that remnants of the divine right of kings may still crack down in a policeman's billy; that the Constitutions of the State and the United States do not change the constitution of human nature; that mere forms of government guarantee neither the character nor the competence of the men in office.

More than common honesty is required in public office and likewise more than common sense. A hundred thousand dollars lost through honest inefficiency is as great a burden to the taxpayers as a hundred thousand dollars lost through conscious fraud. Knowledge is no guarantee of character, we are told. Neither is ignorance. The best of governmental systems may be wrecked by men who do not understand it. After two hundred years of practice in the making of governmental machinery here in North Carolina we propose to go into the training of the men who run it.

The following courses of instruction have grown out of four years of work by staff members of the Institute of Government with officials in city halls, county courthouses and state departments in North Carolina, and have been formally approved by special training school committees and by hundreds of city, county and state officials at a series of open meetings held throughout the state in September, 1937. These men, together with city, county, state and federal officials and teachers of law and government in the colleges and professional schools of North Carolina, will co-operate with the Institute of Government in conducting this training school program.

ALBERT COATES: graduated Smithfield High School, 1913, University of North Carolina, 1918, Harvard Law School, 1923; for twelve years teacher in University of North Carolina Law School, specializing in courses dealing with city, county and state government and its administration; for the last six years working part-time with local, state and federal officials engaged in the administration of the criminal laws in the cities, the counties and the State of North Carolina.

HENRY BRANDIS, JR.: graduated Salisbury High School, 1924, University of North Carolina, 1928, Columbia University Law School, 1931; practiced law in New York City, 1931-3; instructor in taxation at University of North Carolina, 1935-6; from 1933 to 1937 working with city, county and state officials on laws and administrative practices involved in the listing and assessing of property for taxes, the levy and collection of property taxes and on privilege license taxes and special assessments; since 1937 serving as Executive Secretary of the State Tax Classification Amendment Commission.

DILLARD S. GARDNER: graduated Reidsville High School, 1924, University of North Carolina, 1928, University of North Carolina Law School, 1929; practiced law in Marion, 1930-33; from 1933 to 1937 working with city, county and state court officials on the laws and practices involved in the administration of justice in the courts; since 1937 serving as Marshal and Librarian to the Supreme Court of North Carolina.

T. N. GRICE: graduated Columbia, S. C., High School 1924, University of North Carolina, 1928; Certified Public Accountant with Price, Waterhouse & Co. (New York) 1928-34; instructor in municipal accounting at University of North Carolina, 1935-6; from 1934 to 1937 working with city, county and state officials on laws and administrative practices involved in governmental accounting, refunding of debts and other fiscal problems; since 1937 serving with the State Auditor's Office as Certified Public Accountant in charge of the audits of state institutions and departments.

MARION R. ALEXANDER: graduated Asheville High School, 1926, University of North Carolina, 1929, University of North Carolina Law School, 1932; in publicity, magazine and administrative work for University of North Carolina from 1926 to 1934; from 1934 to 1938 working with city, county and state officials in developing a monthly magazine and clearing house of governmental information for federal, state and local units in North Carolina; since 1938 with the Seeman Printery.

HARRY W. McGALLIARD: graduated Chapel Hill High School, 1925, University of North Carolina, 1929; studied at Harvard University Graduate School, 1929-30; graduated University of North Carolina Law School, 1935; for three years a member of the staff of the Institute of Government working in the field of family law, welfare law, and public health law; for the last three and a half years working with city, county and state officials on the laws and practices involved in welfare, health and relief administration in North Carolina.

Criminal Law Administration

Seven statewide institutes from two to ten days in length for city, county, state and federal law enforcing officers have been held in successive years, beginning in 1930. The attendance has steadily increased from around forty to nearly two hundred. Two series of District Institutes have been held: the first in September, 1935, with the state divided into eight districts; the second in September, 1936, with the state divided into five districts; with

LAW ENFORCING OFFICERS

Sixty-one law enforcing officers successfully completed a course of training at a statewide ten-day school for law enforcing officers held by the Institute in Chapel Hill and were presented with certificates by Governor Hoey.

an average attendance of six hundred officers to the series. A ten-day statewide training school for police instructors was held January 5-15, 1937, followed by two series of one-day schools in 1937 and 1938. Many local institutes have been conducted with the co-operation of Judges and Solicitors in counties, cities and towns throughout the state.

Courses arranged for the following official groups: City Police, County Sheriffs, State Patrol and other State agencies; Prosecuting Attorneys and Judges; Probation, Prison, Parole and Pardon Officials. City and County Attorneys, Managers and Commissioners.—Planned by Albert Coates with the cooperation of representatives of the foregoing city, county, state and federal law enforcing agencies.

Topics. The following topics are merely illustrative and will be varied to meet the needs of particular groups attending specific training schools.

CRIMINAL PROCEDURE.

Sources and extent of the criminal law. Law enforcing agencies and territorial limits. Avenues for co-operation. The law of arrests. Methods and practices in making arrests. Limits to search and seizure. Methods and practices in making searches. Limits to self-incrimination. Limits to entrapment. Limits to confessions. Questioning suspects and securing confessions. Limits to confrontation. Fingerprinting arrested persons. Recording of crime scenes. Interviews. Testifying. Report writing. Preliminary hearing. Grand jury. Indictment. Prosecution. Trial. Criminal Courts in North Carolina.

CRIMINAL LAW AND PRACTICE.

Crimes against the person. Homicide: murder, manslaughter. Rape. Assault: simple assault, secret assault, assault and battery, assault with deadly weapon, assault with intent to kill. Riots, routs, affrays and other breaches of the peace. Crimes against property. Larceny, robbery, burglary, arson. Obtaining property by false pretenses. Receiving stolen goods. Embezzlement. Bad check laws. Miscellaneous crimes and laws regulating liquor, narcotics, gambling, prostitution, etc. Investigation of homicide, assault, larceny, robbery, burglary, arson. Automobile theft investigations. Traffic accidents. Traffic laws and safety practices. Traffic problems. License tags. Liquor violations. Narcotics violations. Patrol work. Rules and regulations. Police organization, administration and records. Police problems in small towns. Crime statistics. Remedies for lawless enforcement of laws. Crime prevention. Law and practice of probation, prisons, parole and pardon.

CRIMINAL IDENTIFICATION.

Scientific aids in crime detection. Collecting and transmitting evidence. Illustrations of handwriting identification. Methods of handwriting experts. Obtaining handwriting specimens. Illustrations of typewriting identification. How typewriting is identified. Obtaining typewriting specimens. Paper examination. Ink and pencil writing. Firearms identification. Handling firearms evidence at crime scenes. The laboratory procedure. Glass fractures. Marks and tracks. Inferences from footprints. Identification of footprints. Bloodhounds. Tire tracks. Tool marks. Tooth marks. Searching for blood stains. Method of handling blood stains. Inferences from appearance of blood stains. Origin of the blood stain. Blood tests. Determining whether a stain is blood. Determining whether a stain is human blood. Determining the blood group. Paint stains. Ashes. Cloth. Gathering dirt and debris for examination. Transmitting debris to the laboratory. The laboratory examination. Hairs, fibres and feathers. What the laboratory can tell about hairs and fibres. Metals. Wood. Fingerprinting arrested persons. Advantages of fingerprinting arrested persons. Equipment needed for taking fingerprints. How to take fingerprints. How to utilize the fingerprint files of the FBI. Establishing a small identification bureau. Drawings. Photography. Uses in law enforcement. Principles of police photography. Casting. Plaster of paris casts. Moulage.

As a basis for instruction in the foregoing courses, guidebooks have been prepared on the Law of Arrests, Methods and Practices in Making Arrests, Searches and Seizures, Confessions, the Law of Homicide, Rape, Assault, and other Crimes against the Person, Larceny, Robbery, Burglary, Arson and other Crimes against Property, Methods and Practices of Investigating these Crimes, Traffic Laws and Regulations, Police Organization, Administration, Records, Patrol Work, Interviews, Report Writing, Testifying, Recording of Crime Scenes, Criminal Statistics. Further guidebooks are being prepared on the law and practice of probation, prisons, pardon and parole to round out a comprehensive analysis of all phases of criminal law investigation and procedure in North Carolina.

See pages 3 and 4 for description of laboratory exhibits supplementing foregoing materials for instruction.

Tax Administration

Two statewide institutes for tax supervisors, list-takers and assessors have been held: the first, prior to the tax listing period in 1934; the second, prior to the tax listing period in 1936; with an average of sixty-five of the one hundred counties represented. Three series of district institutes have been held for city and county attorneys and tax collecting officials; the first in September, 1935, with the state divided into eight districts; the second in 1936 with the state divided into five districts; the third in 1937; with an average attendance of two hundred fifty.

Courses arranged for the following official groups: County Tax Supervisors, List-takers and Assessors; City and County Tax Collectors, City and County Attorneys, City and County Accountants, City and County Managers and Commissioners. Planned by Henry Brandis, Jr., with the co-operation of representatives of city, county and state tax officials.

Topics. The following topics are merely illustrative and will be varied to meet the needs of particular groups attending specifis training schools.

LISTING AND ASSESSING OF PROPERTY AND POLLS FOR COUNTY AND CITY TAXES.

The administrative Structure. List takers, assessors, supervisors. Boards of Equalization. State Board of Assessment. Tax-exempt property. Situs of property for taxation. Who must list property. General matters affecting listing—period, place, methods, aids, etc. Practical and legal aspects of listing real estate. Discussion of description. Information on encumbrances, improvements, and transfers. "Permanent listing." Practical and legal aspects of valuing real estate. Statutory elements of value; errors and mistakes; revaluations, etc. Practical and legal aspects of listing personal property—proper questions for list takers to ask; investigation of personalty; other sources of information; credits and deductions; forms, etc. Practical and legal aspects of valuing personal property. Schedules of values for autos, live stock, etc. Industrial machinery. Solvent credits. Property subject to $300 exemption, etc. Review and revisal of assessments. Supervisor's power to change. Notice to taxpayer. Appeal procedure. Making up the tax records (with sample forms). Discovery and listing of unlisted property. Methods, notice, technical aspects, assessment, procedure, penalties, appeals, etc. Property originally assessed by the State Board of Assessment. Procedure for listing and assessing for city and town taxes. Federal and State aids available to the local assessors. Discussion of new statutes, cases, rulings, and practices.

COLLECTION AND FORECLOSURE OF COUNTY AND CITY PROPERTY AND POLL TAXES.

The tax lien—real and personal. Time of attachment. Priorities. Discounts and penalties. Payments—including partial and prepaid. Taxpayer's notes and unit's bonds. Under and over-payments. Bookkeeping problems. The tax books—including form, time, and conditions for delivery. Procedure. Samples. Selling the taxpayer on the prompt payment of taxes. Bills

CITY AND COUNTY ATTORNEYS, TAX COLLECTORS AND FINANCE OFFICERS

City and county attorneys, tax collectors and finance officers, at one of a series of eight district meetings with a total attendance of around four hundred, meet in an institute on laws and practices of taxation and finance administration.

and notices. Advertising campaigns. Installment payments. Personal visits. Financing arrangements, etc. Formal methods of collection (not involving land sales). Levy on personalty, garnishments, etc. Sale of certificates for delinquent taxes. Advertising. Time, place, and manner of sale. Property and taxes subject. Certificates, records, rights, remedies, etc. The Collector's annual settlement. Form, manner, procedure. Tax foreclosure. Election of remedies. Statute of limitations. Parties. Procedure and forms. Costs and fees. Redemption privileges. Joint foreclosures by cities and counties. Special collection problems. Compromises, refunds, release of individual parcels, estates, receiverships, bankruptcies, partnerships, etc. Procedure to contest validity of taxes. Statutory liabilities on governing bodies and tax officials. Tax collection personnel. Discussion of new statutes, cases, rulings, and practices.

THE LEVY OF PROPERTY TAXES.

"Necessary expenses" and "public purposes." Discussion of all North Carolina cases on subject. Limitations on tax rates. Legislative and charter restrictions on city rates. The limit on county rates. "Special purposes" not included within the limited rate, etc. Special tax elections—calling, procedure, and authority. Creditors' proceedings to force levy of taxes. Reducing claims to judgment. Mandamus. Defense of units. Levy of taxes on territory newly included in taxing unit. Discussion of new statutes, cases and rulings.

THE LEVY AND COLLECTION OF SPECIAL BENEFIT ASSESS-MENTS.

Relationship between charter provisions and general laws. City's power to levy—including petitions. Purpose of assessment. Ownership of the street in fee. Charter restrictions, etc. Creation of improvement district and levy of the assessments. Filing of maps. Notice and hearing. Preparation of assessment roll. Percentage borne by city. Appeals. Confirmation, forms, etc. Rights of property owners not appealing originally. Liability for assessments of property owned by governmental agencies. The assessment lien. Time of attachment, character, priorities. Collection of assessments. Records. Advertising. Personal visits. Installment payments. Inability to proceed against personalty. Sale of certificates. Extending time for payment. Statute of limitations. Power of authorities to adjust, compromise or re-assess. Foreclosure of delinquent assessments. Discussion of similarities and dissimilarities to ordinary tax foreclosures. The levy and collection of city and county privilege and franchise taxes. Nature of taxes levied on trades, professions, and franchises. Authority given cities and counties to levy. Restrictions on power of cities and counties—by constitution, revenue act, and other legislation. Adoption of the license ordinance. Specialized licenses—including beer, wine, auto, and dog licenses. Daily, weekly, monthly or seasonal licenses, etc. Collection of license taxes—including billing, advertising campaigns, installment payments, canvassing, levies on personalty, penalties, records, etc. Discussion of new statutes, cases and rulings.

THE LEVY AND COLLECTION OF CITY AND COUNTY PRIVILEGE AND FRANCHISE TAXES.

Nature of taxes levied on trades, professions and franchises. Authority given cities and counties to levy such taxes. Legislative restrictions on the levy of such taxes, with particular reference to taxes which place an illegal burden on interstate commerce. Classification of taxpayers within the same general trade or business. Taxing businesses which have no established office or agency in the taxing unit. Court decisions and Attorney General's rulings construing particular sections of the Revenue Act. Adoption of the license ordinance. Daily, weekly, monthly or seasonal licenses. Methods of enforcing payment of license taxes. Billing. Advertising campaigns. Installment and partial payments. Canvassing and personal contacts. Levies on personal property. Penalties for nonpayment. Criminal prosecutions, etc. Collection of license taxes after year from which they were levied has expired. Collection of two or more licenses from same taxpayer. Collection office records. Specialized licenses, such as beer licenses, automobile licenses and dog licenses. Particular discussion of new statutes, new cases and new rulings of the Attorney General.

As a basis for instruction in the foregoing courses, guidebooks have been prepared on the Collection and Foreclosure of County and City Property Taxes in North Carolina (first edition 1935; revised edition 1938), The Listing and Assessing of Property for County and City Taxes in North Carolina (first edition 1936; revised edition 1938). Guidebooks will soon be available on the subjects of the Levy and Collection of Special Assessments in North Carolina and the Levy and Collection of Privilege License Taxes in North Carolina. Guidebooks are being prepared on the Levy of Ad Valorem Taxes in North Carolina and on North Carolina's Tax Policy 1900-1936, including constitutional and legislative restrictions and taxing powers of counties, cities and towns.

See pages 3 and 4 for description of laboratory exhibits supplementing foregoing materials for instruction.

Finance Administration

Two statewide institutes for finance officers of counties, cities and towns have been held in connection with the Statewide Institutes for all officials heretofore described. One series of District Institutes has been held for city accountants, clerks, treasurers, purchasing agents and other finance officers, with the state divided into five districts. The first Statewide Institute for city, county and state purchasing agents and the first Statewide Institute for municipal finance officers has been held.

Courses arranged for the following official groups: City and County Accountants, Managers, Treasurers, Purchasing Agents, Clerks, and other finance officers. Planned by T. N. Grice with the co-operation of representatives of city, county and state finance officers.

Topics. The following topics are merely illustrative and will be varied to meet the needs of particular groups attending specific training schools.

MUNICIPAL ACCOUNTING AND FINANCE

Note: The courses in the fields of municipal accounting and finance will be varied to meet the needs of cities and towns of different population classes.

Development of duties under general state laws. The Municipal Finance Act, Local Government Laws of 1927 and 1931 and subsequent amendments. Types of accounting systems particularly adapted to cities and towns of different sizes. The necessity of fund segregation and its effect upon accounting for tax revenues, penalties and discounts. Methods of allocating revenues and expenditures to funds. Methods of depositing and safeguarding cash. The necessity for the purpose of a budget. Integrating the budget with actual operations for budgetary control. Methods of obtaining cost data from the general accounting system. Accounting for partial payments on taxes. The cash and accrual bases of accounting and the effect upon accounting for revenues and expenditures. Problems involved in the uniform classification of accounts. The extent to which uniformity is desirable, its limitations and virtues. Adequate inventory records for capital assets. Adequate records for bonded debt and interest payments. The form and content of reports to the governing body. The arrangement and preparation of financial statements. The form and content of public reports and the use of graphs and charts to interpret financial data. Statutory provisions governing the issuance of bonds. The purposes for which bonds may be issued without a vote, legal restrictions as to sale and delivery of bonds, interest rates, maturity dates and amounts, etc. Methods of funding and refunding indebtedness. Statutory provisions. Planning maturity schedules. Advantages of term and serial bonds, advantages of callable bonds, sinking fund requirements, etc. New legislation affecting the duties of accounting and finance officers.

COUNTY ACCOUNTING AND FINANCE

Duties as outlined by County Finance and Fiscal Control Acts and Local Government Act and subsequent amendments. The necessity for fund segregation in the accounting system. Budget preparation and the effect of limitation of tax rate for general purposes. The number and types of funds necessary. Methods of integrating the budget estimates with actual operations for budgetary control. Types of accounting systems adapted to county government. Methods of accounting for partial payments on taxes. Methods of allocating tax collections to funds. Accounting for tax discounts, penalties and interest. The advantages of the cash and the accrual bases of accounting. Safeguarding the collection and depositing of cash. Methods of encumbering appropriation balances when liability is incurred. Financial records to be kept by the Clerk of Court, Sheriff and Register of Deeds. Legal requirements and methods of auditing county officials. The classification of revenue and expenditure accounts in order to get the maximum amount of information. The benefits that can be obtained from uniform accounting. The limitations of uniformity. Types of county functions about which cost data is desirable. The use of cost data in budget preparation and future financial planning. Cost data that can be obtained from the general accounting department. Legal requirements as to public reports. The arrangement of financial statements and the use of graphs and charts to interpret financial information in public reports. Limitations upon the issuance of bonds. When a vote is required. The procedure for sale and delivery of bonds. Legal limitations as to amounts, rates, maturity dates and amounts, etc. Refunding or funding indebtedness—types of bonds that can be issued, limitations upon interest rates, maturities, etc. The procedure for sale, delivery or exchange of bonds. The advantages of term and serial bonds and of callable bonds. Effects of new legislation upon the duties or records of county accounting and finance officers.

PUBLIC PURCHASING

The theory of governmental purchasing. The creation of free and open competition. Methods of finding sources of supply. The effect of commodity standardization. Publicity. Legal requirements as to publicity. The effect of publicity on bidding and prices. Quantity purchases. Selection of commodities to be purchased in quantities. False economy of unwise quantity purchases. The possible effect of recent Federal legislation on quantity discounts. Methods of purchasing. The advantages and disadvantages of purchasing by brand or trade names, upon samples, upon specifications. Information as to the various sources of specifications. Methods of securing quality. Actual performance tests and types of materials fitted to such tests. Analyses. Types of equipment used and methods of analyzing certain commodities. Laboratory tests by vendors and by independent agencies. Certified vendors under federal regulations. Legal restrictions on local purchasing. Requirements as to sealed bids. When informal bids are permitted. The delegation of authority to the purchasing agent. Organization of purchasing procedure. Types of purchasing departments and their organization. The use of departmental requisitions for direct purchases and for supplies issued from storerooms. The procedure for obtaining informal and formal bids. Types of contracts and the advantages of each. Information purchase order should contain. The use of multiple copies purchase orders for financial and informational purposes. Provisions for emergency orders. Receiving procedure. Control over checking quantities and prices. Paying procedure. Approving invoices for payment. Coordination of purchasing and general accounting department. Operation of storerooms and warehouses. Methods of appropriating for stores department. Relation of stores department to purchasing department. Organization and layout of storerooms. Receiving, inspection and checking procedure. Permanent inventory records. Purchasing records. Financial records. Information records. The use of vendor, price and commodity files and indices. Cross indexing and coordinating information records. The use of market quotation records in making spot purchases and determining trends.

As a basis for instruction in the foregoing courses, guidebooks have been prepared on Refinancing of Bonded Debt of Counties, Cities and Towns in North Carolina and chapters completed in guidebooks for Accountants, Treasurers, Clerks and other finance officers. Guidebooks are being prepared on Public Purchasing in Cities, Counties and the State; Preparation of City, County and State Budgets; Uniform Accounting and Reporting Procedure for Counties, Cities and Towns; Powers and Duties of Accountants, Clerks, Treasurers, Purchasing Agents and other Finance Officers of Counties, Cities and Towns.

See pages 3 and 4 for description of laboratory exhibits supplementing foregoing materials for instruction.

Administration of Justice in the Courts

Two statewide institutes for court officials have been held in connection with the statewide institutes for all officials heretofore described. One series of district institutes has been held for sheriffs, one for clerks of court, and one for registers of deeds, with the state divided into five districts and a total attendance of two hundred twenty-five sheriffs, deputy sheriffs and newly elected sheriffs, ninety-seven clerks and deputy clerks of court, and eighty-six registers and deputy registers of deeds.

Courses arranged for the following official groups: Clerks of city, county and state courts; Sheriffs; Registers of Deeds; Justices of the Peace and other Judicial Officers; State and Local Bar Officials.—Planned by Dillard S. Gardner with the co-operation of representatives of city, county, state and federal court and bar officials.

Topics. The following topics are merely illustrative and will be varied to meet the needs of particular groups attending specific training schools.

SHERIFFS.

Status of office. Structure and organization of office. Oaths—bonds—deputies, their appointment and powers. Transfer of office to successor. Office,

SHERIFFS

Pictured above are sheriffs and deputies at one of three series of eight district meetings for sheriffs, clerks of court and registers of deeds, with more than two-thirds of these officials in attendance at the meetings.

supplies and equipment—budget—county commissioners. Qualifications and disqualifications of Sheriff. Resignation, vacancy and removal. Compensation—salary, and fees—how governed. Criminal and civil liability. Civil Duties of Sheriff. Receiving process. Handling on receipt—entries. Service of process. When no act is to be performed. Subpoenas of witnesses and jurors. Summonses and notices. Special forms of personal service. Corporations, foreign and domestic, public. Infants and insane. Persons ill. Time of service—liability. When some act to be performed. Claim and delivery—

including levy, bond, etc. Attachment, including levy, sale, bond, etc. Arrest and bail, including bond, etc. Executions, including levy, exemptions, sale, etc. Return of process. Time of return. Contents in particular cases. Accounting for funds. Legal aid in complex returns. As court-room officer, including jury duties. Drawing jury, before and during court—keeper of key to jury boxes. Assisting grand jury. Assisting petit jury. Assisting court—serving instanter process—keeping order in court-room. Timely topics of current interest.

As a basis for instruction in the foregoing course, chapters of guidebooks have been completed for Sheriffs. Complete guidebooks are being prepared in the Civil Powers and Duties of Sheriffs.

REGISTERS OF DEEDS.

Status of office. Structure and organization of office. Oaths—bonds—deputies, appointment and powers. Transfer of office to successor. Office, supplies, and equipment. Qualifications and disqualifications. Attendance at office. Vacancy and resignations. Compensation—salary or fees—laws governing. Criminal and civil liability of Register. Duties of officer. Principal duty: recording instruments relating to title, etc. Minor duties: marriage licenses, clerk to board, vital statistics, record of tax and federal liens, official bonds, pension roll, etc. Recording, filing and indexing. Recording. Methods of recording—transcribing old records—divisions. Selection of records, supplies. Use of forms—encouraging use of forms. Recording plats—repairing plat records—standardizing plats and photostatic recording—filing of duplicates—methods of transcribing old plats. Indexing. Types of indexes—re-indexing—checking. Temporary indexes—types—time and methods of permanent indexing. Reference to files. Filing. Systems—disposition of old files. Supplies. Selection of binders, paper, ink, etc.—value of check of records for this. Factors—cost, durability, legibility, etc. Analysis of particular duties. Cancellation of mortgages and deeds of trust. Methods permitted. Foreclosure entries. Register's duty. Duties as Clerk to Board. Keep minutes—check claims—prepare vouchers—prepare reports, etc.—relation to accountant. Vital Statistics Record. Necessity of binding—value of indexing—methods. Registration and custody of official bonds. Methods used. Annual Report of Clerk. Recording and publishing—where recorded.

As a basis for instruction in the foregoing course, guidebooks have been prepared on the Powers and Duties of Registers of Deeds in North Carolina.

CLERKS OF THE SUPERIOR COURT.

Status of office. Structure and organization of office. Oaths. Bonds. Assistants and deputies. Transfer of office to successor—audits and inventories. Office and equipment—budget—county commissioners. Personal attendance of Clerk at office—vacations, leaves. Disqualifications of Clerk—procedure. Resignation, vacancy and removal. Compensation of Clerk—salary or fees—laws governing. Criminal and civil liability of Clerk. Duties of Clerk. Judicial and ministerial duties distinguished. Judicial duties. Probate matters. Special proceedings. Statutory, judicial powers of special nature. Civil actions. Estates. Wills. Guardianships. Trusteeships. Partition. Sale of land for assets. Re-investment of trust estates. Revocation of appointments of fiduciaries. Particular statutory special proceedings. Arbitration of school tax disputes. Condemnation proceedings in eminent domain. Recording, indexing and filing—systems—efficiency and economy. Issuing process—subpoenas, summonses, attachments, claims and deliveries. Making required reports. Taking acknowledgments, etc. Court-room duties. Appeals. Checking computations of interest, totals, etc. in accounts. Receiving dockets, reports, etc. from justices of the peace. Receiving election returns from local officials. Receiving certain public welfare reports such as those in adoptions, sterilizations, etc.

As a basis for instruction in the foregoing course, chapters of guidebooks have been completed for Clerks of Court. Complete guidebooks are being prepared on the Powers and Duties of Clerks of Court.

SERVICES OF THE INS

TO CITY, COUN
AND STATE OFFICI

COMPARATIVE STUDIE
of the structure and
workings of govern-
ment in the cities,
counties and state
of
NORTH CAROLINA

set forth in — GUIDEBOOKS

Taught in — Schools and Conferenc

Demonstrated in — Governmental Laborator
and Demonstration Offi

LEGISLATIVE SERVICE
to inform officials
citizens and schools
LAWS IN THE MAKING
AND LAWS ALREADY
MADE

Through

CLEARING HOUSE
between city halls,
couty court houses,
state departments,
federal agencies,
the school room, and
the people of
NORTH CAROLINA

Through

'ITUTE OF GOVERNMENT

TO CITIZENS	TO SCHOOLS
Study and Discussion Groups	Supplementary Texts
Institutes for Public Affairs Committees	Training Courses for Civics Teachers
Governmental Laboratory and Demonstration Offices	Governmental Laboratory and Demonstration Offices

Periodic Summaries of Daily Bulletins	Periodic Summaries of Daily Bulletins
Summary of New Public Laws	Summary of New Public Laws
Summaries of New Trends in Local Legislation	Summaries of New Trends in Local Legislation
State & District Conferences for Interpretation of New Laws	State & District Conferences for Interpretation of New Laws

Digests of Supreme Court Decisions and Rulings of Atty-Gen. and State Depts.	Digests of Supreme Court Decisions and Rulings of Atty-Gen. and State Depts.
Bulletins on New Federal Laws, Programs, and Rulings	Bulletins on New Federal Laws, Programs, and Rulings
Monthly Magazine and Special Studies	Monthly Magazine and Special Studies
Federal and State Services to Local Units	Federal and State Services to Local Units
General Informational Service	General Informational Service

JUSTICES OF THE PEACE.

Criminal jurisdiction. Analysis of crimes punishable by not over $50 or 30 days. Territorial limits. Relation to Mayors', Recorders', County, and Superior courts. Procedure. Records. Appeals. Civil jurisdiction in Contract. Analysis of claims where sum demanded does not exceed $200 and title to realty is not in controversy. Territorial limits. Authority after judgment. Power in special cases. Relation to higher courts. Procedure. Records. Appeals. Civil Jurisdiction in tort. Analysis of claims where value of property in controversy does not exceed $50. Power in ejectment, attachment, claim and delivery, and actions on witness tickets. Relation to higher courts. Procedure. Record. Appeals.

As a basis for instruction in the foregoing course, chapters of guidebooks have been completed for Justices of the Peace. Complete guidebooks are being prepared on the Powers and Duties of Justices of the Peace.

CONFERENCES OF JUDGES, SOLICITORS AND LOCAL AND STATE BAR OFFICIALS.

Constitutional status of courts. Provisions regulating status, structure, organization, and powers of courts. Provisions regulating judges and judicial officers. Court of impeachment. Supreme Court: Organization. Powers.— Original jurisdiction. Appellate jurisdiction—of facts—of law. Supervisory jurisdiction. Advisory jurisdiction. Power to Disbar (licensing power). Rule-making power. Relation to other courts. Superior Courts: Criminal powers as related to Justices of the Peace, Mayors' Courts, Statutory, inferior courts. Civil powers as related to Clerks of Superior Court, in probate matters and special proceedings, equity jurisdiction, contract jurisdiction, tort jurisdiction. Clerk of the Superior Court: Probate jurisdiction. Special proceedings jurisdiction. Civil action jurisdiction. Jurisdiction under special statutes. Ministerial duties. Justice of the Peace: Powers. Criminal and civil. In contract and in tort. Mayors' Courts: Organization and power. Statutory—inferior courts: Organization. Constitutional limits defined. Types of courts:—civil—criminal—general—special purpose. Commissions and administrative agencies: Organization. Extent to which judicial powers may be granted by statute. Powers. Relation of all inferior courts to superior court: necessity that right of appeal to superior and to supreme court be preserved in creating inferior courts. Extent to which inferior courts may have concurrent powers with superior court.

As a basis for discussion in the foregoing conference, studies are being prepared on the activities of state and local bar associations. Nearing completion is a detailed study of The Evolution of North Carolina's Judicial System and Plan of Court Organization from the Constitution of 1868 to the Present Day.

See pages 3 and 4 for description of laboratory exhibits supplementing foregoing materials for instruction.

Legal and Governmental Aspects of Public Works Administration

Public works officials met in 1932 in connection with the organization of the Institute. Subsequent meetings have been held periodically since the inauguration of the federal public works program in 1933, and bulletins have been issued to public works officials. In the meantime, research has been progressing on the Legal and Governmental Aspects of Public Works Administration. Chapters have already been completed on Legal Aspects of (1) Street and Sidewalk Construction and Maintenance, (2) Construction, Maintenance and Inspection of Public Buildings, (3) Sewers,

Drains and Water Courses; (4) Liability of City for Injuries Caused by Conditions of the Premises—Public Buildings, Parks, and Playgrounds; (5) Liability of Municipal Corporations for Damage to or Loss in Value of Property Caused by Grading or Improving Streets; (6) Tort Liability of Municipality in Connection with the Operation of an Electric Light System; (7) Tort Liability of City for Injuries Suffered by Prisoners as Result of Failure of City to Properly Maintain and Supervise Jails; (8) The Laws Governing Fire Administration.

Courses arranged for the following officials: Public Works Commissioners, Building Inspectors, Public Utility Directors, City Attorneys, City Engineers, Superintendents of Streets, Buildings, Water, Sanitary Departments and Sewage Disposal plants.

Topics. The following topics are merely illustrative and will be varied to meet the needs of particular groups attending specific training schools.

PUBLIC WORKS

Liability of municipal corporations for injuries caused by defects or obstructions in streets and other public ways: Construction and upkeep of streets as a governmental function. The duties, in general, of a municipal corporation with respect to its streets. Streets and ways to which the city's duty of exercising reasonable care extends. Notice a city must have had of the dangerous condition of one of its streets in order to be held liable for an injury resulting therefrom. Actual notice. Constructive notice. Circumstances for which municipalities have, and have not been held negligent with respect to the condition of their streets. With reference to obstructions. Excavations. Dangerous bridges. Culverts. Snow and Ice on the streets and sidewalks. Other defects in the surface of streets. Other defects in sidewalks. Falling objects. Street termini. Intersections. Absence of lights.

When contributory negligence is a defense: When the plaintiff has no knowledge of the defect and no reason to expect it. When the plaintiff has no knowledge of the existence of a defect but by the exercise of ordinary care might discover and avoid it. When the plaintiff knows of the defect or has noticed it in the past. Use of streets by blind men, unattended, as contributory negligence. Speeding as contributory negligence. Violation of an ordinance as contributory negligence. Other instances of contributory negligence. Other defenses somewhat related to contributory negligence. Insulated negligence. Imputed negligence. Avoidance of liability by city by showing that another cause as well as its negligence contributed to the injury. Fellow servant rule. Failure of the plaintiff to give notice of his claim to the governing body of the city as a defense. Order of liability when both an individual and a city have been negligent with respect to a dangerous condition in a street. Evidence.

Liability of municipal corporations for damage to or loss in value of property caused by grading or improving streets: Basis of city's liability where damage caused by failure to do the work with ordinary skill and caution. Situations in which property may be damaged or lessened in value because of grading, recovery being precluded because the work was done properly. When a city is guilty of actionable negligence in grading a street such that an adjoining property owner is entitled to recover damages. Liability for gross abuse of discretion. Ratification.

Waterworks and utilities: Sewers, drains and water courses. Choosing source of supply. Protecting water shed. Condemnation of reservoir sites. Eminent domain and pipe lines. Purification of water. Liability for supplying impure water. Municipal power to control and regulate. Private sewers and drains. Stream pollution. Natural water courses. Surface water. Electric light plants and other public utilities. Power of city to operate. Eminent domain. Regulation of utility rates. Tort liability of municipality in connection with the operation of an electric light system.

Building inspection, public buildings, parks and playgrounds: Building inspection as a governmental function. Powers and duties of building inspectors. Liability for negligence. Fire chief as building inspector. Laws governing inspection. Condemnation of buildings. Buildings for governmental purposes and proprietary purposes. City halls. Jails. Markets. Auditoriums. Liability for unsafe condition. Supervision of playgrounds. Defective playground equipment as basis for liability.

Fire fighting and fire prevention: A guidebook on the laws governing fire administration and the powers, duties and liabilities of firemen is being prepared by the Institute under the supervision of the State Fire Marshal, the President of the North Carolina Firemen's Association and the President of the North Carolina Fire Chiefs' Association.

See pages 3 and 4 for description of laboratory exhibits supplementing foregoing materials for instruction.

Legal and Governmental Aspects of Public Health, Welfare and Relief Administration

Two statewide institutes for Welfare, Health and Public Works Officials have been held in connection with the statewide institutes for all officials heretofore described. One series of district institutes has been held for welfare officers in their capacity as Juvenile court and probation officers.

Courses arranged for the following official groups: City, county and state health officials, city, county, state and federal welfare officials, juvenile court officials, probation, parole and prison officials.—Planned by Harry W. McGalliard with the co-operation of representatives of city, county, state and federal health and welfare officials.

Topics. The following topics are merely illustrative and will be varied to meet the needs of particular groups attending specific training schools.

PUBLIC HEALTH.

Organization of health department. The State Board of Health. The State Laboratory of Hygiene. Bureau of Sanitary Engineering and Inspection. County Boards of Health. The county physician or health officer. The county quarantine officer. Municipal health officer. Local and district health departments. Sanitary districts. Civil liability of Public Health officers. Rule making powers. Nuisances or conditions dangerous to the public health. Infectious diseases. Sanitary regulations. Sterilization of mental defectives. "Occupational Diseases" and the Workmen's Compensation Act. School health work. Inebriates, drug addicts, and insane persons. Convicts. Regulation of dairies, dairy products and bakeries. Inns, hotels and restaurants. Vital statistics.

PUBLIC WELFARE.

Growth and development of public welfare in North Carolina. Organization of a state welfare department. The county superintendent of public welfare. General duties of the county superintendent. Poor relief. Old age assistance, aid to dependent children. Aid to needy blind. Unemployment relief. Mother's Aid. The insane. Sterilization. Pardon, parole and probation. Juvenile courts. Juvenile court procedure. Juvenile court treatment of cases. Child labor. Adoption. Children of unmarried parents. School attendance. The crippled and physically defective. Laws regulating commercial amusement. Investigations 'in the cause of distress." Workmen's compensation act. Veteran's benefits. Working conditions for women. Drugs and narcotics.

Venereal diseases. Marriage laws. Divorce, annulment and alimony laws. Investigation of penal institutions.

As a basis of instruction in the foregoing courses, guidebooks are being prepared on Laws Relating to the Powers and Duties of Welfare Officers, Laws Relating to the Powers and Duties of Health Officers, Jurisdiction and operation of Juvenile and Domestic Relations Courts.

See pages 3 and 4 for description of laboratory exhibits supplementing foregoing materials for instruction.

Elections

One statewide institute has been held for election officials, and institutes have been held in counties throughout the state prior to elections.

Conferences arranged for the following official groups under the leadership of the Chairman of the State Board of Elections: Members of State and County Boards of Elections, Precinct Registrars and Judges, and members of State and County Executive Committees of various political parties.

Topics. The following topics are merely illustrative and will be varied to meet the needs of particular groups attending specific training schools.

GENERAL ELECTIONS (STATE, COUNTY, AND TOWNSHIP) AND PRIMARIES

Powers and Duties of State Board of Elections. Powers and Duties of County Boards of Election. Precinct Election Officials, including Registrars and Judges, assistants and their qualifications. Oath of Office. Method for filling vacancies. Registration, including nature and time and place. Qualifications for voting, including exclusions, requirements. Hearing challenges on election day and oaths and affirmations. Registration on election day. Absentee ballots, including persons entitled to use, applications, forms, certificates, signing and voting, time limit for receipt, opening, counting and reporting, challenges and posting names. Conducting the Election: Personnel, including registrars, judges, assistants, markers, watchers and challenges. Vacancies in precinct offices. Polling place, including arrangement of voting enclosure, necessary equipment, booths, boxes and ballots. Other supplies furnished by county boards. Equipment arranged locally. Powers and duties of officials on election day. Opening the polls. Persons allowed within voting enclosure. Voting. Closing the polls. Canvassing and reporting ballots, including counting the ballots and sealing the ballot boxes. Precinct returns, including signing poll books and accounting for ballots. The county canvass. Meeting of county board. Attendance of registrar or judge. Canvassing results. County abstracts. Returns to State Board. Report to Secretary of State. Articles to bring to County canvass. Compensation and Bills for supplies. Corrupt practices: Statement of campaign contributions and expenses. Acts declared misdemeanors. Acts declared felonies for election officials and for any persons. Rules of State Board of Elections. Forms: Items furnished by state and by counties. General oath of registrar. Certificate of removal. Registration oath. Report of registration. Oath for challenged electors. Notice of absentee voters. Election day oath. Report of ballots. Record of absentee ballots. Expense statement.

MUNICIPAL AND SPECIAL ELECTIONS AND PRIMARIES.

General laws applicable to municipal and special elections, including the 1901 Act (elections) and the Australian Ballot Act of 1929 (primaries and elections).

General laws applicable to cities subject to act, embraced in Municipal Corporations Act of 1917 (primaries).

Variations by city charter and special act relating to particular cities. Rules for construing and determining which governs as between general

State-wide laws and as between State-wide laws and local acts for a particular city.

As a basis for instruction in the foregoing courses, guidebooks have been
prepared on the Election Laws of North Carolina (first edition 1933, second
edition 1934, third edition 1937), and a supplementary guidebook for municipal election officials (1937).

See pages 3 and 4 for description of laboratory exhibits supplementing foregoing materials for instruction.

City Government

Two institutes have been held for mayors and city councilmen.

Note: Inasmuch as these officials are charged with the supervision
and control of practically all municipal governmental functions,
this course will include a survey of the subject matter of all the
foregoing courses in addition to a study of powers and duties
peculiar to city governing bodies.

*Courses arranged for the following officials: Mayors, City Councilmen, City
Managers and City Attorneys.*

CITY GOVERNMENT

Organization plans of towns and cities. Plan A: Mayor and city council
elected at large. Plan B: Mayor and city council elected by districts and at
large. Plan C: Commission form of government. Plan D: Mayor, city council and city manager. Variations in organization plans. Governmental functions and activities of towns and cities and the machinery for the performance of these governmental functions: Supervision and control of Criminal
Law Administration, Tax Administration, Court Administration, Finance
Administration, Public Works Administration, Health, Welfare and Relief
Administration. Ordinance making power. Statutory grant of power. How
exercised. Form of ordinance. Publication of ordinance. Police Power.
Power delegated by State. Licensing power. Matters affecting public safety,
public health, morals and general welfare. Fiscal Administration. Relation
to local government commission. Power to levy taxes. Purposes of appropriations. Debt limitation amendment. What constitutes a public purpose.
What constitutes a necessary expense. Bond issues. Municipal property.
Power to acquire and alienate. Purposes for which property may be ac-
quired. Disposition of property. Public or private sale. Methods of acquiring
and disposing of property. Power to Contract. General powers. Terms of
contract. Power to bind successors. Trading with members of governing
body. Municipal Liability in Tort. Nature of liability. Acts or omissions of
officers or agents. Defects or obstructions in streets. Defects or obstructions
in sewers, drains and water courses. Condition and use of public buildings.
Liability for negligence of agents and employees. Governmental functions
and proprietary functions. Municipal officials and employees. Power to ap-
point and discharge. Civil Service systems. Pensions. Requirement of surety
bonds. Relation of city government to county, state and federal government.

As a basis for instruction in the foregoing courses, guidebooks have been
prepared in the fields of Criminal Law Administration, Tax Administration,
Finance Administration, Court Administration, Election Laws, and Federal-
State-Local Relationships. Guidebooks and texts are being prepared on
Municipal Liability in Tort, Legal Aspects of Public Works Administration,
Public Health, Welfare and Relief Administration, and the Powers and
Duties of city governing bodies.

See pages 3 and 4 for description of laboratory exhibits supplementing
foregoing materials for instruction.

County Government

Two institutes have been held for county commissioners and county managers.

Note: Inasmuch as these officials are charged with the supervision and control of practically all county governmental functions, this course will include a survey of the subject matter of all the foregoing courses in addition to a study of powers and duties peculiar to county governing bodies.

Courses arranged for the following officials: County Commissioners, County Managers, County Attorneys.

COUNTY GOVERNMENT

Forms of county government. County commissioners form. Modifications of county commissioners form. County managers form. Power to levy taxes and incur debt. Powers and duties. Right to make contracts. Control of county buildings. Power to acquire and dispose of property. Making provision for poor. Supervision and control of law enforcing machinery. Supervision and control of Criminal Law Administration, Tax Administration, Court Administration. Public Works Administration, Health, Welfare and Relief Administration, Fiscal Administration. Budget-making. Relation to local government commission. Purposes of appropriations. Debt limitation amendment. What constitutes public purpose. What constitutes a necessary expense. Bond issues. Licensing power. Police Power. Relations to county Board and Officials: Sheriff, Registers of Deeds, Clerk of Court, Board of Elections, Board of Education, Board of Charities and Public Welfare, A. B. C. Board, Board of Health, County Attorney, Treasurer, Auditor, Coroner, Superintendent of Public Welfare, Farm Agent, Home Demonstration Agent, Surveyor. Relation of county government to city, state and federal government.

As a basis for instruction in the foregoing courses, guidebooks have been prepared in the fields of Criminal Law Administration, Tax Administration, Finance Administration, Court Administration, Election Laws, and Federal-State-Local Relationships. Guidebooks and texts are being prepared on County Liability in Tort, Legal Aspects of Public Works Administration, Public Health, Welfare and Relief Administration, and the Powers and Duties of County Commissioners.

See pages 3 and 4 for description of laboratory exhibits supplementing foregoing materials for instruction.

State Government

A meeting of state officials in September, 1938, marked the beginning of the State division of the Institute, with the Governor and seventy-four state department and division heads present to pledge their participation in the program.

Note: Many state department heads have inaugurated the practice of informal staff conferences. Some are developing these staff conferences into consecutive periods of instruction. A few are developing systematic training programs. For example; a two-day institute for accountants, auditors and budget officers of state departments and institutions was held in June, 1938, by T. N. Grice, Certified Public Accountant of the State Auditor's staff, R. G. Deyton, Assistant Director of the Budget, and other officials of the State Auditor's office, under the auspices of the

STATE OFFICIALS

State department and division heads approve the program of the Institute of Government and pledge their co-operation.

Institute of Government, with around seventy-five officials in attendance.

As an aid in developing these systematic training programs the Institute of Government is co-operating with state department heads and their chief assistants in outlining (1) the development of each state agency, (2) its present powers and duties, (3) its methods and practices in exercising these powers and performing these duties, (4) the interrelationships of units within each department, (5) the interrelationships of each department with other state agencies and with city and county units.

Members of many departments have indicated a desire for a comprehensive course in state government and are co-operating with the Institute of Government in working out plans to this end. The complexity of the functions of state government and the need for a training course in this field along the plan outlined above is demonstrated by the growth in state departments and agencies from four in 1776, to 29 in 1900, to 62 in 1920, to more than 100 departments, commissions and agencies today.

The following course of instruction, designed for accountants and auditors, illustrates the type of training courses to be worked out under the leadership of state department heads with the co-operation of the Institute.

GOVERNMENTAL ACCOUNTING.

The field of governmental accounting. The purpose of governmental accounting. Characteristics of governmental accounting and commercial accounting. Funds: Meaning of funds. Types of funds. Accounts of funds. Procedure of different funds. Expendable Revenue Funds: Nature. "Budgetary" and "Proprietary" accounts. Encumbrances. Cash and accrual basis. General ledger accounts. The Budget: Place in accounting system. Budget procedure. Budgetary accounts. Revenues. Appropriations. Subsidiary ledgers, Revenues: Classification. Accounting for revenues. Cash receipts: Classification. Accounting for receipts. Expenditures: Appropriations. Encumbrances. Classification, accounting and audit of expenditures. Disbursements: Accounts of the treasury. Function of the treasury. Inter-fund transactions. Petty cash. Revenue funds and the fiscal period: Accounts affected by fiscal period. Reserves. Unappropriated surplus. Fund statements. Bond funds: Scope and purpose. Operation. Accounting procedure. Balance sheet. Special Assessment funds: Purpose and nature. Method of operation. Improvement expenditures. Trust and agency funds: Nature. Classification. Funding of trust monies. Operation and accounting procedure. Pooling of investments. Trust fund statements. Working capital funds: Stores and service departments. Purpose and scope. Procedure of operation. Cost elements and price basis. Accounting procedure. Job accounts: Purpose and scope. Procedure. Elements of cost. Labor. Material. Overhead. Working capital fund accounts in general office. Statements of operations. Sinking funds: Meaning and scope. Accounting procedure. Fixed assets and liabilities: Classes. Accounting methods. Subsidiary records. Fund balance sheet and financial reports: Purpose. Preparation and content.

See pages 3 and 4 for description of laboratory exhibits supplementing foregoing materials for instruction.

Federal, State, Local Relationships

Three Statewide Institutes have been held by the Legislators' Division including city councilmen, county commissioners, state legislators and congressional representatives; the first, in September, 1932; the second in June, 1933; the third, in June, 1935; with an average attendance of six hundred. One series of district Institutes was held in 1937. Prior to the meeting of the General Assembly in 1935 the Legislators' Division of The Institute of Government invited representatives of the counties, cities and towns to appear before the newly elected legislators to discuss their respective legislative programs. Subsequent to the sessions of the General Assembly in 1933 and 1935 and 1937 Institutes were held for the interpretation of state and federal legislation to officials and units affected by it.

Courses arranged for City Councilmen, County Commissioners, State Legislators, Federal Representatives and other city, county, state and federal administrative officials.—Planned by Marion R. Alexander with the co-operation of representatives of the foregoing groups.

Topics. The number of agencies of the federal and state government furnishing services and operating in close relation to city and county governments is too numerous to list the subjects of discussion in connection with all. Examples have been chosen and other agencies are merely listed.

NEW DEAL AGENCIES.

Works Progress Administration: Grants to city and county projects. Types of projects eligible. Small works. Non-construction. Requirements. Public sponsor. Location on publically-owned land. Contribution by city or county. Employment. Relief rolls. Registrations with state and local agencies. Procedure. Assistance to youths—NYA. Student Aid. Work on federal projects. Job guidance and placement. Apprentice training. Community activities.

Other agencies: Public Works Administration. Soil Conservation Service. Civilian Conservation Corps. Rural Electrification Administration. Tennessee Valley Authority. Farm Security Administration. Reconstruction Finance Corporation. Home Owners Loan Corporation. Federal Housing Administration. Farm Credit Administration.

STATE-FEDERAL ENTERPRISES (Federal Aid System)

Federal Highway Aid. Grants to states. Annual federal aid grants—requiring matching with state funds. Direct emergency grants—not requiring matching with state funds. Eligible projects. Roads on federal aid highway system. Elimination of grade crossing hazards. Extensions into and through municipalities. Secondary or "feeder" roads in rural areas. Roads in national forests, parks, and reservations. Administration. State plan and administration. Federal approval and inspection. Local requests and petitions for projects—to state highway commission. Preferred projects. Closing of gaps in the federal aid highway system. Elimination of traffic hazards, particularly railroad. Improvement of projects of particular use to other government agencies. Roads correlating and supplementing other existing transportation facilities. Improvement of roadsides. Reconstruction designed to reduce maintenance costs and decrease future costs. Small projects providing the maximum of human labor.

Other agencies: Land Grant Colleges. Agricultural Experiment Stations. Agricultural Extension Service. Soil Conservation. Agricultural Adjustment Administration. Forest Fire Control and Reforestation. Vocational Education and Rehabilitation. National Guard. State Employment Service.

REGULAR FEDERAL DEPARTMENTS AND BUREAUS.

National Bureau of Standards. Weights and measures inspection. Governmental purchasing. Testing of public purchases. Public utility standards. Traffic and safety. Safety codes. Planning and zoning. Building and plumbing codes. Making results available.

Other agencies: Department of Commerce. Department of Agriculture. Department of the Interior. Department of Labor. Department of the Treasury. Department of Justice. War Department. Navy Department. Miscellaneous Boards and Commissions.

STATE DEPARTMENTS.

Local Government Commission. Inspection and approval of plans for bond and note issues. Sale of bonds and notes. Notices to buyers. Placing of advertisements. Notice of debt service requirements and maturities. Checking and approval of tax anticipation loans. Information and advice in setting up revolving funds. Assistance in securing sinking funds and public deposits. Selection of depository banks. Selection of sound securities. U. S. and State bonds. Bonds of unit or other N. C. units. Approval of surety bonds. Checking of reports. Notices to units whose sinking funds do not meet requirements. Assistance with refinancing and refunding operations. Information and advice. Preparation of plans. Negotiations with creditors. Checking of reports and annual statements. Inspection and approval of budgets. Auditing contracts and systems. Advice and scope as to nature. Approval of contracts. Form for reports. Examination and approval of new systems. Selection of accountants. Lists of eligibles. Passing on qualifications. Information and materials. Codification of local government law. Forms for budget and annual report. Rulings and general counsel.

Other agencies: Municipal Board of Control. Attorney General. State Treasurer. Department of Revenue. Division of Purchase and Contract. State Highway and Public Works Commission. Department of Public Instruction. Board of Education. School Commission. State Board of Health. State Board of Charities and Public Welfare. State Institutions for Juvenile Dependents. State Commission for the Blind. State Department of Labor. Department of Agriculture. Department of Conservation and Development. Highway Patrol. National Guard. Commissioner of Pardon and Parole. Secretary of State. Insurance Commissioner. Utilities Commission. Alcoholic Beverages Control Board. Probation Commission. Bureau of Identification. Rural Electrification Authority. Unemployment Compensation Commission. Industrial Commission. Library Commission.

As a basis for instruction in the foregoing courses, guidebooks have been prepared on Federal Services to the State, Counties, Cities and Towns; State Services to Counties, Cities and Towns. Guidebooks are being prepared on Legislative and Administrative Practices and Procedures in City Halls, County Courthouses and the State Capitol.

See pages 3 and 4 for description of laboratory exhibits supplementing foregoing materials for instruction.

Laws Affecting Married Women's Rights

Course arranged primarily for public affairs committees and other members of women's organizations.—Planned by Harry W. McGalliard with the cooperation of representatives of women's clubs.

Topics. The following topics are merely illustrative and will be varied to meet the needs of particular groups attending specific training schools.

WOMAN AND THE LAW IN NORTH CAROLINA.

Marriage laws. The capacity to marry. Age of consent. Parent's written consent. Kinship. Interracial marriage. Bigamous marriage. Marriage license. Registrar's duties. Form of marriage ceremony. Common law marriage. Annullment of marriage. Divorce laws. Divorce bed and board. Absolute divorce. Grounds for divorce. Defences to divorce action. Who may obtain divorce. Alimony. Married women's property rights. Personal property. Real property. Husband's rights in wife's property. Wife's earnings. Dower. Curtesy. Homesteads. Married women's contracts. Business relations between husband and wife. Husband's liability for support of wife. Injuries to the person and character. Labor laws. Criminal laws as affecting the relationship of husband and wife. Custody of children. Suffrage and office holding. Jury service.

As a basis for instruction in the foregoing course, a guidebook has been prepared setting forth the history of the laws governing the Legal Rights of Married Women, from Colonial Times to the Present.

See pages 3 and 4 for description of laboratory exhibits supplementing foregoing materials for instruction.

Students and Teachers of Civics and Government in the Schools

The need to bridge the gap between government as it is taught in the schools and as it is practiced in the city halls, county courthouses and state capitol grows out of the fact that with rare exceptions the high schools, colleges, and professional schools of North Carolina are each year graduating around 20,000 boys and girls, knowing something of textbook civics but little of practical government; knowing how to read a page of Latin but not knowing how to read their own municipal balance sheet; knowing how to find their way around Rome but not knowing how to find their way around their own city hall, county courthouse or state capitol. As a result thousands of officials are going into office without an opportunity to acquaint themselves with their powers and duties or the methods and practices of their predecessors. Hundreds of thousands of citizens are going to the ballot box without adequate understanding of the workings of their governmental institutions.

Institutes for students and teachers of civics and government in the schools will equip them to interpret the current developments in government and its administration and focus them in the classroom at the classroom hour. Four State wide Institutes have been held for Superintendents, Principals and Teachers of Civics and Government; the first, in September, 1932; the second, in June, 1933; the third, in November, 1934; the fourth, in June, 1936. One series of district institutes has been held, in November, 1935, with the state divided into eight districts, and a total attendance in excess of one thousand.

TEACHERS OF CIVICS AND GOVERNMENT

Courses arranged for students and teachers of civics and government in the schools.

Topics. The following topics are merely illustrative and will be varied to

TEACHERS OF CIVICS AND GOVERNMENT

Teachers of civics and government, at one of a series of eight district meetings held throughout the State with a total attendance of more than a thousand, participate in the Institute's program.

meet the needs of particular groups attending specific training schools.

Governmental Structure. Forms of city government. City officials. Powers and duties of governing bodies. County government. County commissioners form. County manager form. State departments and agencies. Interrelationship of state departments. Interrelationship of city, county, state and federal governmental agencies. Comparison of powers of city councilmen, county commissioners and state legislators. *Tax Administration.* Sources of revenue. Right of city, county and state to levy taxes. Property tax. Poll tax. Sales tax. Income tax. License taxes. Gasoline tax. Franchise taxes. Restrictions on taxation. Purposes for which tax money may be spent. *Criminal Law Administration.* City, county, state and federal agencies for the investigation of crime and apprehension of criminals. Criminal law in action: arrest, detention, trial, punishment, probation, pardon and parole. Functions of grand jury, prosecuting attorney, trial jury, judge and parole commissioner. Juvenile delinquency and crime prevention. *Court Administration.* Structure of the court system in North Carolina. Justices of the peace. Mayor's courts. Recorder's courts. Juvenile courts. County courts. Superior courts. The supreme court. Court procedure—the progress of a law suit. *Health, Welfare and Relief Administration.* Functions and interrelations of city, county and state departments of health, public health laws. City, county and state welfare departments. Social security legislation. *Public Works Administration.*

As a basis for instruction in the foregoing course, textbooks on student government have been completed on city, county, state and federal government and their interrelationships.

See pages 3 and 4 for description of laboratory exhibits supplementing foregoing materials for instruction.

Public Affairs Committees of Citizens' Organizations

The need to provide the machinery for putting the people in touch with their government and keeping them in touch with it grows out of the fact: that citizens for the most part do not become acquainted with the practical workings of their government in high school and college classrooms; that after they leave school they do not have any systematic way of keeping in touch with it as they busy themselves with the varied tasks of making a living; that in times of stress and strain they try to cut the climbing costs of government by organizing taxpayers' leagues and citizens' committees; that these leagues and committees are ill-equipped to find the facts they need to know; that even when they find the facts in their own local units they are crippled by the lack of a clearing house for the exchange of comparative governmental information with other units. These feverish organizations come and go with every depression. They have once more largely disappeared; but they live long enough to point out with all the stinging freshness of demonstrated truth that foresight costs less than hindsight and that citizens can be constant sources of help instead of hindrance to their officials and save thousands of dollars for themselves by attending to their government as they attend to their business.

CITIZENS' ORGANIZATIONS

Members of citizens' organizations approve the program of the Institute of Government at a statewide meeting and pledge their co-operation.

Four statewide institutes for representatives of citizens' organizations. of men and women have been held in connection with the institutes for officials: the first, in September, 1932; the second, in June, 1933; the third, in November, 1934; the fourth, in June, 1935.

Course arranged for public affairs committees of civic organizations and other interested citizens.

Topics. The following topics are merely illustrative and will be varied to meet the needs of particular groups attending specific training schools.

CITIZENS

Forms of city and county government: Powers and duties of governing bodies of cities. Commissioners form of county government. County Manager form. Expansion of governmental functions. Interrelationship of state departments. Interrelationship of city, county, state and federal governmental agencies. Comparison of powers of city councilmen, county commissioners and state legislators. *City, county, state and federal tax administration:* Sources of revenue. Right of city, county and state to levy taxes. Listing and assessing of property taxes. Poll tax. Sales tax. Income tax. License taxes. Gasoline tax. Franchise taxes. Restrictions on taxation. Purpose for which tax money may be spent. Election laws. *Criminal law administration:* City, county, state and federal law enforcing agencies. Criminal law in action: arrest, detention, trial, punishment, probation, pardon and parole. Functions of grand jury, prosecuting attorney, trial jury, judge and parole commissioner. Treatment of juvenile delinquents. Prevention of crime. *Court administration:* Structure of the court system in North Carolina. Justices of the peace. Mayor's courts. Recorder's courts. Juvenile courts. County courts. Superior courts. The supreme court. Court procedure—the progress of a law suit. *Health, welfare and relief administration:* Unemployment compensation. Workmen's compensation. Functions and interrelations of city, county and state departments of health, public health laws. City, county and state welfare departments. Family law. Social security legislation. *Public works administration.*

As a basis for instruction in the foregoing course, textbooks are being prepared on city, county, state and federal government and their interrelationships.

See pages 3 and 4 for description of laboratory exhibits supplementing foregoing materials for instruction.

Commonsense of Co-operative Effort

In 1663 the Charter from the Crown created North Carolina as a single governmental unit. This single governmental unit we have divided into 100 counties. On this dividing framework of the counties we have laid the subdividing framework of the township. On this subdividing framework of the township we have laid the overlapping framework of the city and town. Across this complicated governmental pattern we have thrown a crazy quilt of special districts.

There may have been a time when cities, counties and the State were isolated and insulated from each other and the outside world; but today their rapidly expanding functions have produced interlocking, overlapping and conflicting relationships to the point that there is hardly a major governmental problem they do not share with each other and the federal government. They are partners in the administration of the criminal law; in the administration of justice in the courts; in the administration of taxation, accounting and finance; of health, welfare and relief; of utilities and public works.

Here in North Carolina city, county, state and federal officials working on the same problems for the same people in overlapping governmental units are coming together as partners in a great co-operative program: governmental research, public service training, demonstration laboratory and clearing house of information. The advantages of co-operative effort are plainly apparent. Cities, counties, state departments and federal agencies in North Carolina are integral parts of the same governmental structure and the problems of one cannot be understood without an understanding of their relations to the problems of the other. To illustrate: city police, county sheriffs, and increasingly state patrolmen operate under similar laws of arrests, search and seizure, evidence, criminal investigations, criminal law and procedure. Research for one is research for all; guidebooks for one are guidebooks for all; training schools and instruction staff for one are training schools and instruction staff for all; laboratory and clearing house of information for one are laboratory and clearing house for all. City and county tax collectors, attorneys and finance officers likewise operate under similar laws and employ similar procedures and techniques. Research for one group has been research for all groups; guidebooks on tax collection and foreclosure are used in city halls, county courthouses and state tax departments alike; the same instruction staff, laboratory and clearing house serves all. Likewise in the administration of justice in the courts. Likewise in health, welfare, relief and public works. Likewise the Institute has provided a legislative service keeping officials in city halls, county courthouses, and state departments in daily touch with bills affecting their interest introduced in the General Assembly, summarized resulting legislation for them at the end of the session and acquainted them with Attorney General's rulings and Supreme Court decisions interpreting those laws and defining the powers and duties of units and officials.

Not only does the co-operative approach cut by two-thirds the costs that would accrue to cities, counties and the state from operating duplicating programs; the same research that goes into guidebooks, instruction in training schools, and demonstration laboratories for officials will go into textbooks, training schools and demonstration laboratories for the public affairs committees of citizens groups and for teachers and students of civics and government in the schools.

CPSIA information can be obtained
at www.ICGtesting.com
Printed in the USA
BVHW081514061118
532319BV00013B/1903/P